OUR UNITED STATES OF AMERICA

COLORING & ACTIVITY BOOK

e Playmore Waldman Bug Logo® is a registered trademark of Playmore Inc., Publishers and Waldman Publishing Corp., New York, New York

Published by Playmore Inc., Publishers and Waldman Publishing Corp., New York, New York

Printed in Canada

Pocahontas, an Indian Princess, saved the life of John Smith,
an early settler.

1616

Later, Pocahontas married John Rolfe and visited England.

Samoset was a chief of the Pemaquid Indians. In March 1621 he greeted the colonists at Plymouth Rock.

Samoset and his people lived in peace with the Pilgrims for 50 years.

Benjamin Franklin 1706-1790 was an inventor, author, printer,
publisher, scientist, businessman, statesmen,
philosopher and diplomat.

When Benjamin Franklin was only twelve, he became
a printing apprentice.

Here is a typical colonial scene, but is it? How many things wrong with this picture can you find?

HOW MANY ERRORS CAN YOU FIND?

After you have found all the errors, color this scene.

George Washington was born in 1732 — in this simple cottage
in Westmoreland County, Virginia.

George Washington

When Washington was sixteen he began work as a
surveyor —measuring land.

Washington served bravely during the French and Indian War.

Crispus Attucks, an African American, was the first American to die during the Boston Massacre – March 5, 1770.

He was the leader of a group that opposed the British soldiers.
This was a key event that led to our American Revolution.

Paul Revere was a great silversmith as well as a patriot.
Which teapot is different?

Every morning little Beth went out to collect eggs for her mother. One day she saw that eggs had been laid in the center or a square island in the middle of a square pond. How did Beth reach the islands?

(See next page for Answer)

Answer: Beth placed the planks in the way they are shown in the picture below. That is how she reached the island and collected the eggs for her mother.

Help George Washington get to the French fort to deliver his message.

START HERE ⇧

Betsy Ross made our flag. Her daughter watched as she worked.

General George Washington visited Betsy Ross as she
worked on the flag.

ALABAMA SURPRISE!

Follow the dots to see a flying ship!
Rockets are designed in Alabama.

Alabama

6 ●

5 ●

● 7

U
S
S
A

● 4

● 8

2 ●

● 3

● 9

● 10

1 ●   ● 13

● 12

● 11

USA
Alabama
USA

ALIFORNIA — COLOR BY NUMBER

Hollywood, California is the main source of movie and television programs in our country. Color this cool Hollywood dude below!

California

1 — Green 2 — Yellow 3 — Red 4 — Pink
5 — Purple 6 — White

Thomas Jefferson was born in 1743. He was the author of the
Declaration of Independence and later went on to become President.

Daniel Boone 1734-1820 was a skilled woodsman. He led pioneers across the Allegheny Mountains.

HIDDEN ENEMIES

Help Daniel Boone find **9** Indians hiding in the forest.

Molly Pitcher brought water to the thirsty Revolutionary soldiers during the Battle of Monmouth in 1778.

When her husband was wounded she took his place and fought
the rest of the battle.

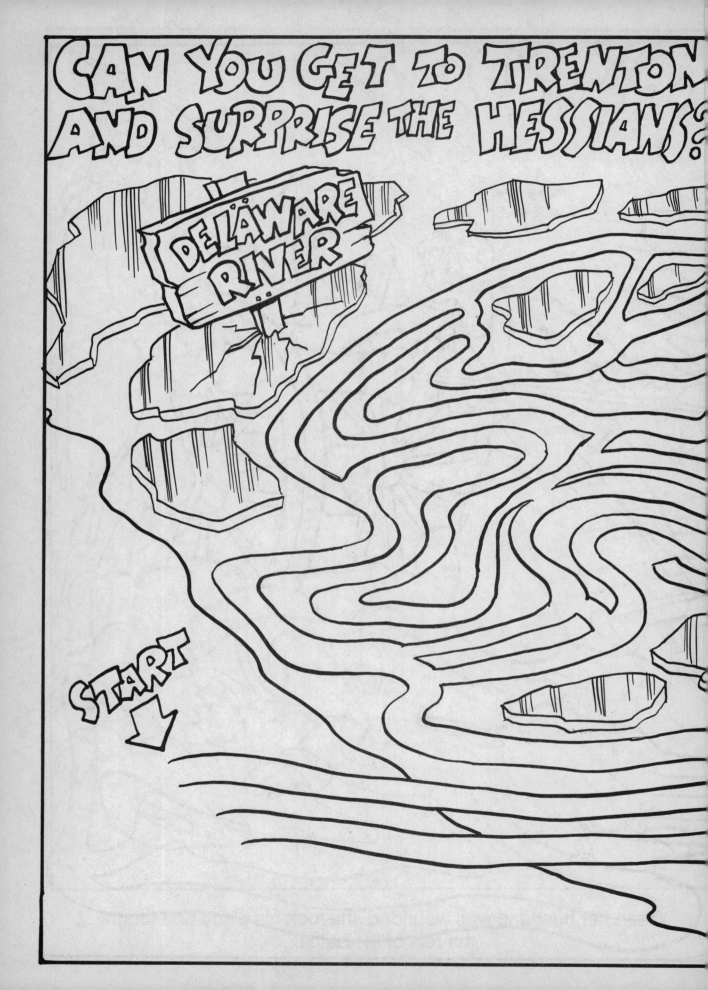

FIRST NATIONAL BANK

PHILADELPHIA 1791

Alexander Hamilton 1757-1804 became the first Secretary of the Treasury. Hamilton helped the young nation to have a stable economy.

Jefferson engineered the Louisiana Purchase and sent Lewis and Clark to explore the new land.

DESERT DOT TO DOT

Much of Arizona is desert. Cactus in the Arizona deserts can grow to a height of 50 feet and an age of 300 years. Connect the dots to see the cactus!

Robert Fulton 1765-1815 was the inventor of the steam ship.

DIAMOND FIND

Arkansas

Arkansas is the only diamond producing state.
Help the diamond miner find **5** hidden diamonds!

Eli Whitney 1765-1825 invented the cotton gin and cotton growing became one of the young nation's profitable industries.

Harriet Tubman, an African American, became the leading conductor of the "underground railroad" that helped slaves escape to freedom.

She made over 19 trips and helped rescue over 300 slaves, never losing a soul. She was never caught.

Harriet Beecher Stowe 1811-1896 wrote *Uncle Tom's Cabin*, a book that helped teach people how wrong slavery was.

Clara Barton 1821-1912 founded the American Red Cross.

Abraham Lincoln was a poor boy who grew up in a log cabin.

Lincoln as a young man had no paper and pencils. He used a board to write on with charcoal. He studied by the light of an old fireplace.

As a young man he worked as a rail splitter.

Abraham Lincoln, one of our greatest Presidents, freed the slaves.

DOWNHILL MAZE

Colorado is a western state with many high mountains.
Can you help the skiers get down the mountain?

Colorado

FIND THE DIFFERENCES

Connecticut was founded by Puritans. Can you find at least **8** differences between these two Puritans?

Connecticut

Dorothea Dix 1802-1807 was superintendent of women nurses in Washington D.C. during the Civil War.

After the war she worked to establish state mental hospitals and
effect prison reforms.

Ulysses S. Grant was the Civil War general that led the North to victory.

Robert E. Lee was the military commander of the Confederacy.
He was a courageous general.

SUNSHINE MATCH
Florida, the sunshine state, produces 75% of America's fruit. Which of each group of 3 below matches most closely the picture in the first box?

PEANUT MAZE

Georgia leads the nation in peanut production. Georgia native Joel Harris wrote about "Br'er Rabbit." Can you help this rabbit get through the peanut maze?

Georgia

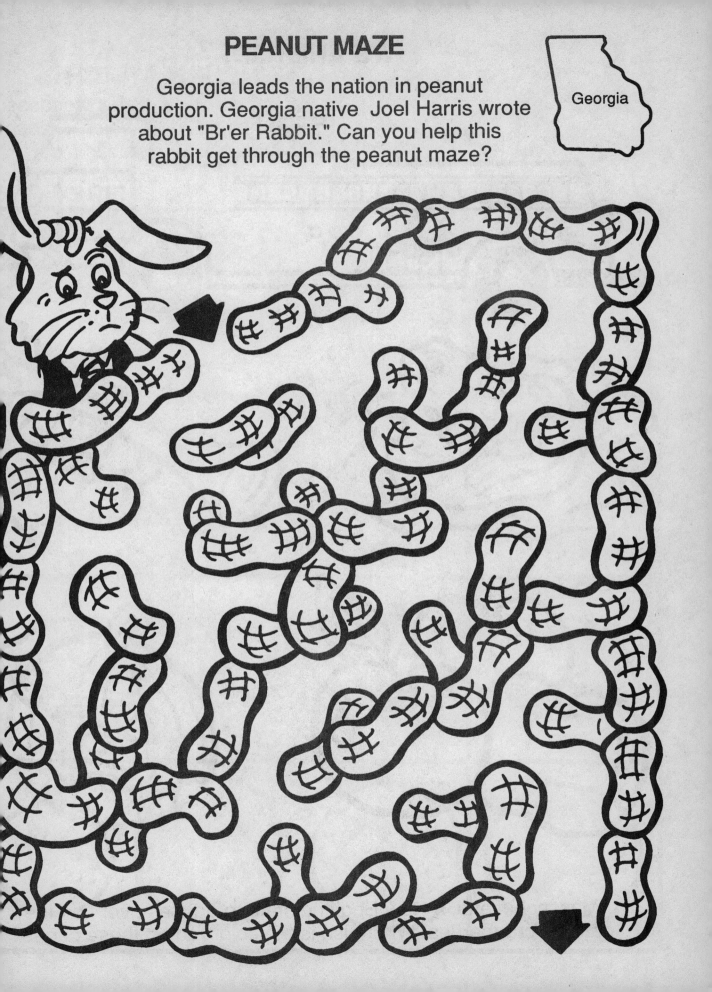

WE ARE RED!

Massachusetts, a New England state, produces over half the nation's cranberries. What else is the color red on these pages?

5

Massachusetts

6

7

8

9

10

STOP

Frederick Douglass was born in 1817.
He was a slave who worked hard to learn to read and write.

After he became free, Douglass spoke and wrote
for equality and liberty for all people.

PRESIDENT SHADOW MATCH

This 16th President moved to Illinois when he was 21 and was elected President in 1860. Match the shadow with the President below.

Illin

INDIANA APPLES

Indiana was the home of John Chapman, "Johnny Appleseed," who devoted his life to planting apple trees over 100,000 square miles. How many apples can you find below?

ndiana

POTATO JUMBLE

Idaho is known for potatoes. How many potatoes can you find in the jumble below?

IOWA DOT TO DOT

Iowa is known as the "bread basket" of the United States. **Follow the dots** to see some of the food Iowa produces.

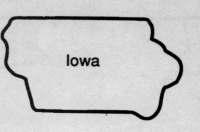

Iowa

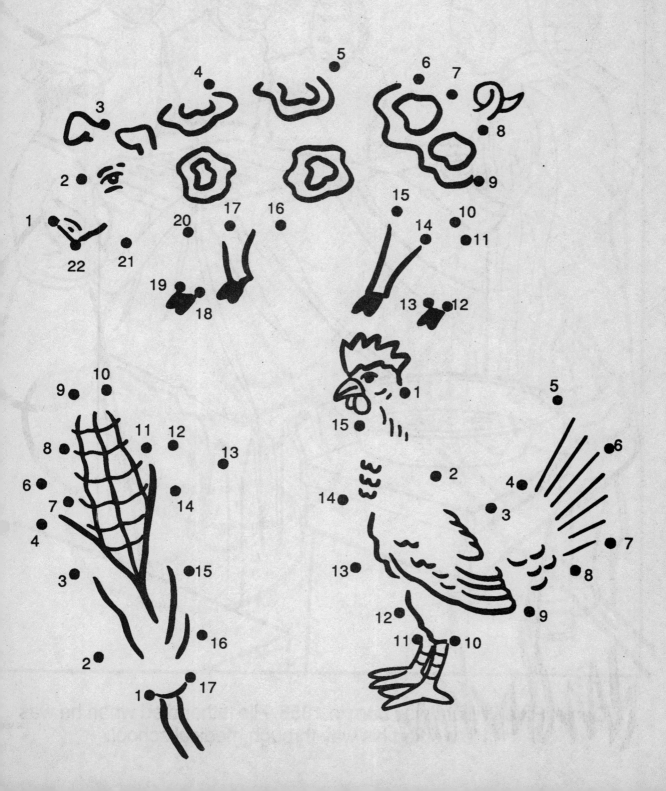

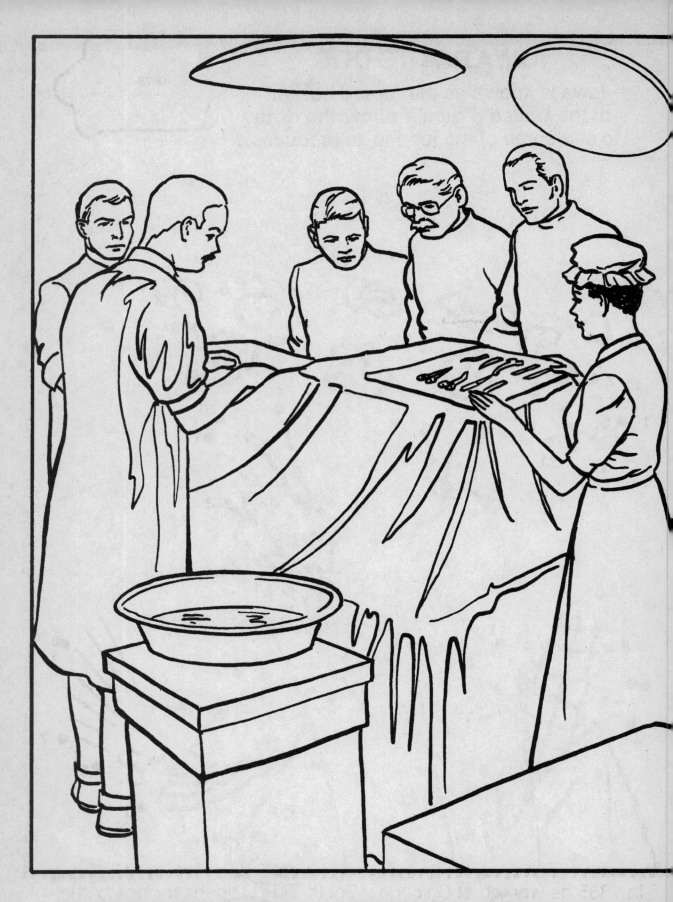

Daniel Hale William was born in 1855. His father died when he was 11. He worked his way through medical school.

In 1885 he worked at Chicago's South Side Dispensary, one of the few places African American doctors were allowed to practice. He became the first surgeon to operate on a human heart.

KANSAS AT THE CENTER

A point in Kansas is the center of the United States.
Draw a line connecting points A and D.
Draw another line connecting points B and C.
These lines would intersect in Kansas.

Kansas

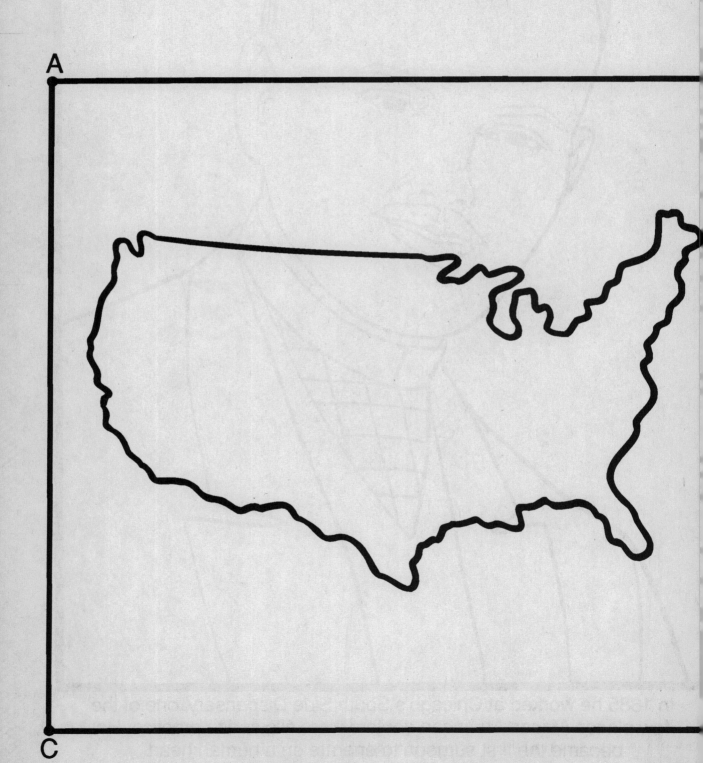

DOT TO DOT SURPRISE!

N. Dakota

S. Dakota

When the first explorers found the Dakota territory, they saw large herds of the animal above. **Follow the Dots** to see this large animal.

Answer: Buffalo

OKLAHOMA

Oklahoma resembles a deep dish frying pan. Find Oklahoma below!

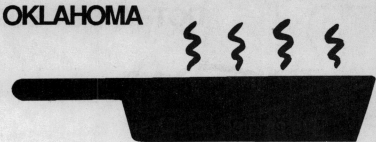

A

B

C

D

E

F

G

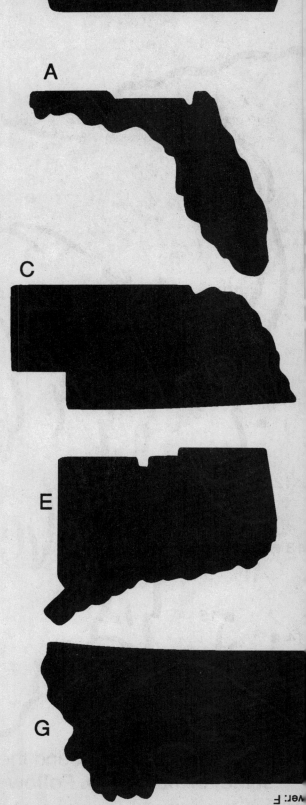
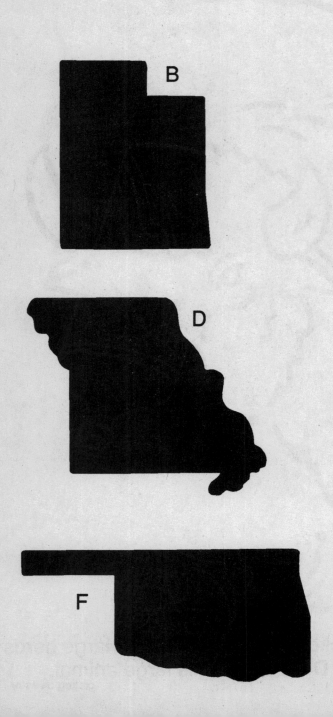

LOUISIANA CELEBRATION

Louisiana

MARDI GRAS

Over a million party-goers march through the streets of Louisiana every year during Mardi Gras. They wear wild costumes. Color this Mardi Gras mask.

This code was developed by soldiers
to send messages to their friends.

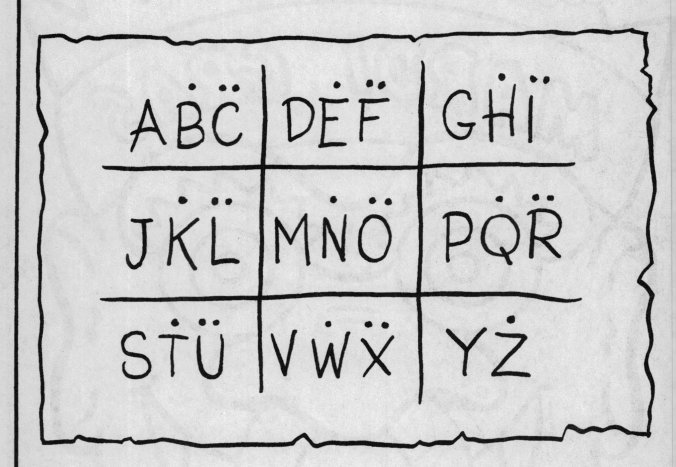

Notice that there are three letters in each section. The last section has only two. The second letter of each group has one dot over it. The third letter of each group has two dots over it. The first letter of each group has no dots.

So in this code   HAVE FUN = ⌐˙ ⌐ ⌐¨ ⌐   ⌐¨ ⌐˙˙ ⌐

Decode this message:

⌐ ⌐˙˙ ⌐   ⌐ ⌐˙ ⌐   ⌐ ⌐ ⌐˙˙ ⌐ !

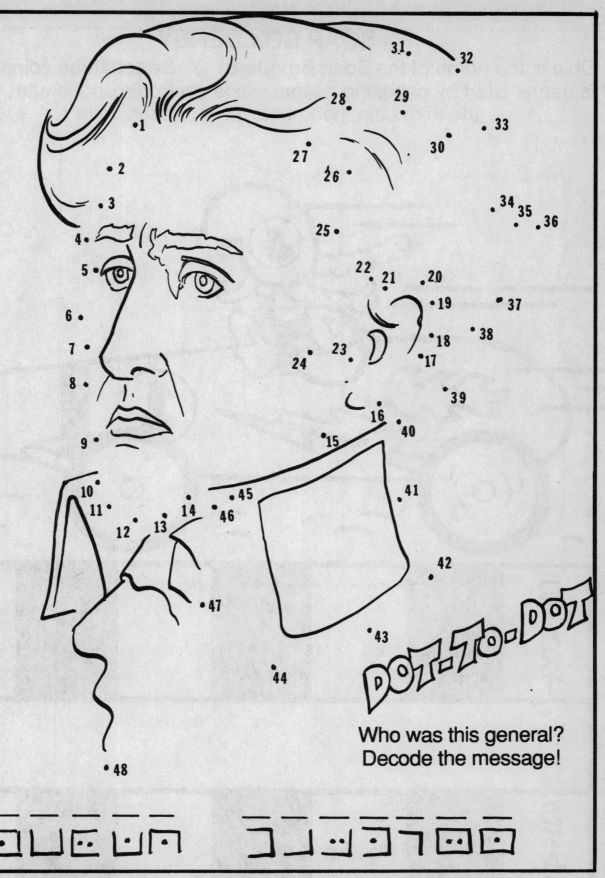

Who was this general?
Decode the message!

1767-1845 The time or era he lived in is now named after him.
He symbolized the rise of the New West and the victory of the
common man.

SOAP BOX DERBY

Ohio is the home of the Soap Box Derby. You need three coins to play this game. Start by choosing a lane. Place your coin on the start. Now flip the third coin; heads moves 2 spaces, tails 1.

The first one to reach the checkered flag space wins!

Ohio

FIND THE TWINS
Maine is known for its delicious lobsters
Find the 2 lobsters that most closely match

Maine

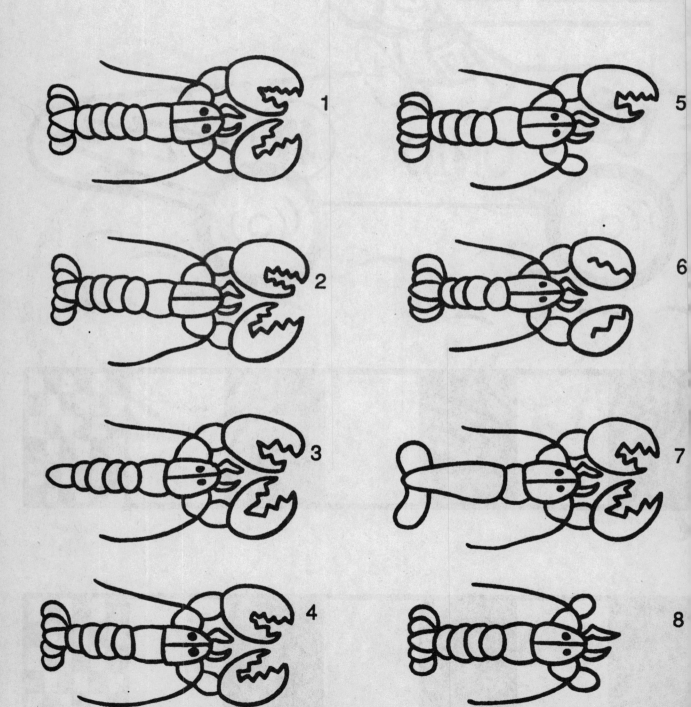

1

5

2

6

3

7

4

8

CIRCLE FIND

Maryland

Maryland is the number one oyster producing state.
Color in the scene above and find at least **10** circles.

Minnesota is called the land of 1,000 lakes. Lumberjacks made up tale
of how these lakes were formed. Some say a giant lumberjack
named Paul Bunyan had a giant blue ox named Babe.

When Babe walked his giant hooves made big holes
which rain filled, forming lakes. Color Babe
and Paul Bunyan.

Minnesota

Samuel Morse 1791- 1872 invented the telegraph. He was also a famous artist.

MORSE CODE

Morse invented a code made up of dots and dashes. You can use this code by tapping with a stick or using a flashlight or whistling.

Morse code is an alphabet. Each letter is made of (short) dots and (long) dashes. The dash is three times as long as the dot.

A .−	J .−−−	S ...	1 .−−−−
B −...	K −.−	T −	2 ..−−−
C −.−.	L .−..	U ..−	3 ...−−
D −..	M −−	V ...−	4 ....−
E .	N −.	W .−−	5 .....
F ..−.	O −−−	X −..−	6 −....
G −−.	P .−−.	Y −.−−	7 −−...
H	Q −−.−	Z −−..	8 −−−..
I ..	R .−.		9 −−−−.
			0 −−−−−

CAN YOU DECODE WHAT PATRICK HENRY SAID?

"—— •• ••• — • ——• •

•—•• •• —••• • •——• ——•••

——— •—• ——• •• ••• • •

—•— —• •—• —• • •—• — ••• !"

CAN YOU DECODE WHAT PAUL REVERE SAID?

"— •••• • —••• •—• •• — •• ••• •••

•— •—• • ——— —•• •• ——

WHAT'S MISSING?

Michigan is the capital of the Automobile Industry.
Color the cars above that have missing parts, red.
Color the remaining cars all different colors.

Michigan

MONTANA MATCH!

"Big Sky Country" was the site of Custer's Last Stand. Which of each group of three below matches most closely the picture in the first box?

Montana

MISSISSIPPI IS THE "MAGNOLIA STATE"!

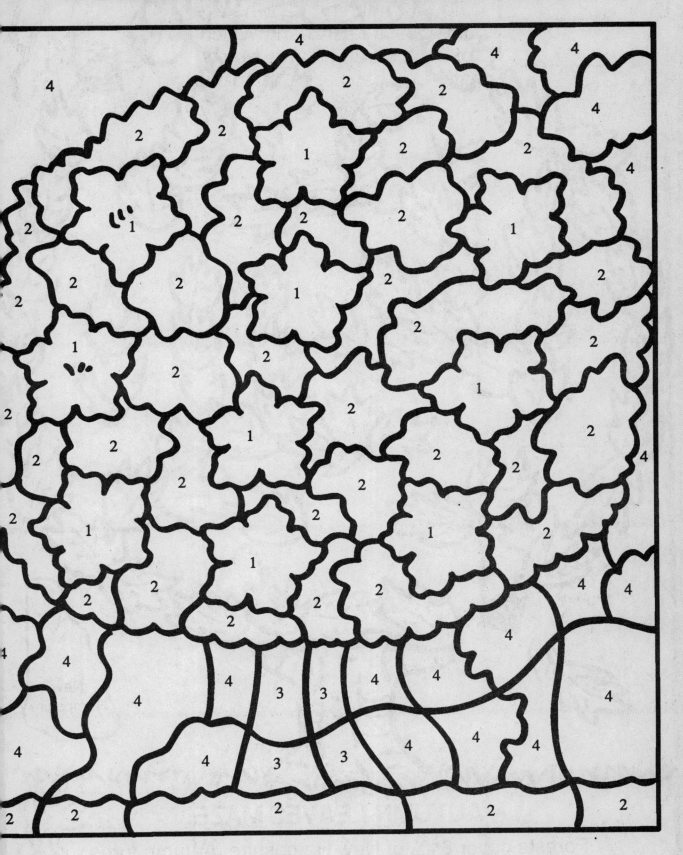

Color by Number the Magnolia Tree.
1—Pink 2—Green 3—Brown 4—Blue

New Hampshire

AUTUMN LEAVES MAZE

Forests cover 84% of New Hampshire. Autumn turns the leaves beautiful colors. Can you get through this autumn leaves maze?

New Jersey has more people per square mile than any other state. Can you find a chef, nurse, doctor, football player, and fireperson in the crowd.

Thomas Alva Edison 1847-1931 was America's greatest inventor.

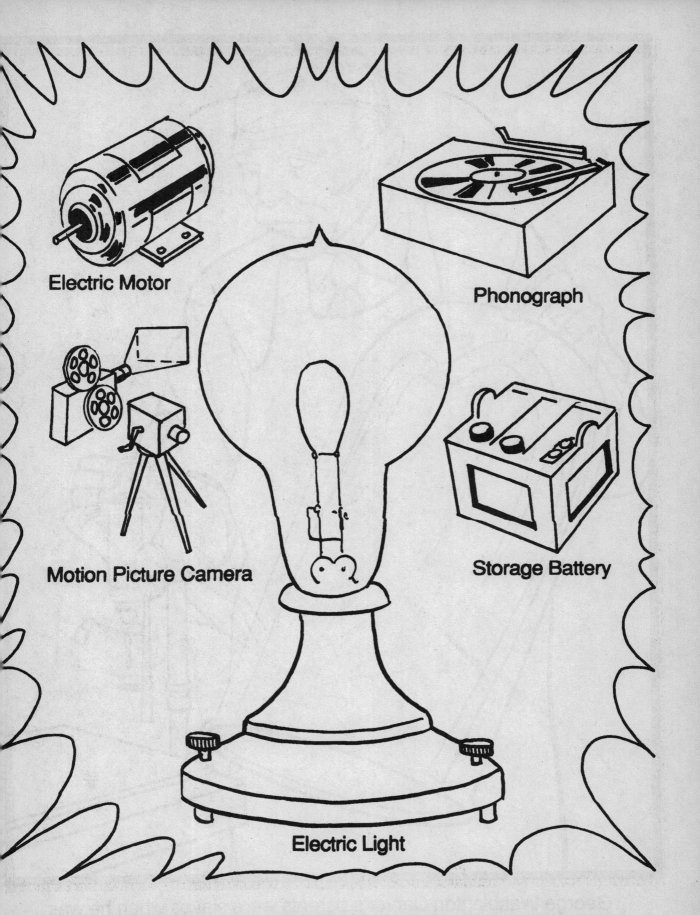

Electric Motor

Phonograph

Motion Picture Camera

Storage Battery

Electric Light

His inventions have had great impact on the way we live our lives.

George Washington Carver's parents were slaves when he was born in 1860.

He studied botany and found 300 uses for peanuts and helped farmers.

There are 50 states in the United States of America. Can you find your state on the map? Can you name any others? Check your answers below.

49

1. Delaware
2. Pennsylvania
3. New Jersey
4. Georgia
5. Connecticut
6. Massachusetts
7. Maryland
8. South Carolina
9. New Hampshire
10. Virginia
11. New York
12. North Carolina
13. Rhode Island
14. Vermont
15. Kentucky
16. Tennessee
17. Ohio

18. Louisiana
19. Indiana
20. Mississippi
21. Illinois
22. Alabama
23. Maine
24. Missouri
25. Arkansas
26. Michigan
27. Florida
28. Texas
29. Iowa
30. Wisconsin
31. California
32. Minnesota
33. Oregon
34. Kansas

35. W. Virginia
36. Nevada
37. Nebraska
38. Colorado
39. N. Dakota
40. S. Dakota
41. Montana
42. Washington
43. Idaho
44. Wyoming
45. Utah
46. Oklahoma
47. New Mexico
48. Arizona
49. Alaska
50. Hawaii

MISSOURI — HOME OF MARK TWAIN

Color by Number to see what Tom Sawyer has his friend doing.
1—White 2—Brown 3—Green 4—Yellow 5—Black 6—Blue
7—Pink 8—Red

WHAT'S WRONG?

braska, the "Cornhusker state," produces 10% of the nation's corn.Find at least **6** things wrong with the farm scene above.

Nebraska

Cyrus Hall McCormick 1809-1884 at the age of 22 built the first practical reaping machine.

Luther Burbank 1849-1926 was an American plant breeder. He created many new trees, flowers, fruits and vegetables.

Alexander Graham Bell 1847-1922 invented the telephone.

WHAT'S MISSING?

Nevada is a very dry state where desert
creatures live. Look at each picture number 1
and in each of the following pictures draw
in the missing parts.

Nevada

1

1

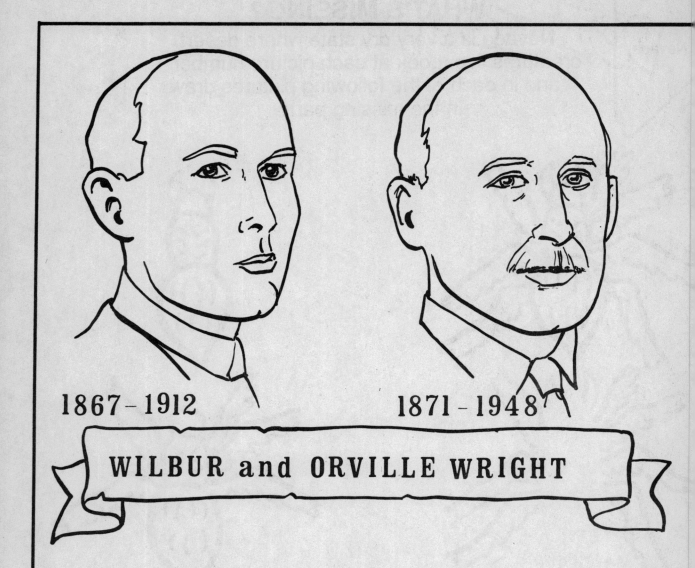

1867–1912

1871–1948

WILBUR and ORVILLE WRIGHT

These brothers started the Wright Cycle company. They made, sold and repaired bicycles. Follow the Dots to see their great invention.

DOT-TO-DOT

December 17, 1903 — Kitty Hawk, North Carolina

WE CAN'T FLY!

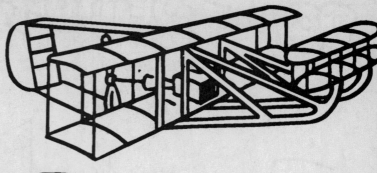

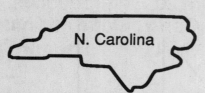

Kitty Hawk, North Carolina was the site of the first manned flight. Which items below can't fly?

1

2

3

4

5

6

7

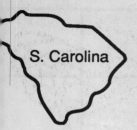

S. Carolina

SOUTH CAROLINA QUIZ

South Carolina leads the world in cotton production. Clothes are made from cotton. Can you draw a line between the product and where it comes from?

A

B

C

D

1 MILK

2

3 NEWS

4

NEW YORK

The United States symbol of liberty, the 151 feet tall
Statue of Liberty, is located in New York. France gave
it to our country in 1884.

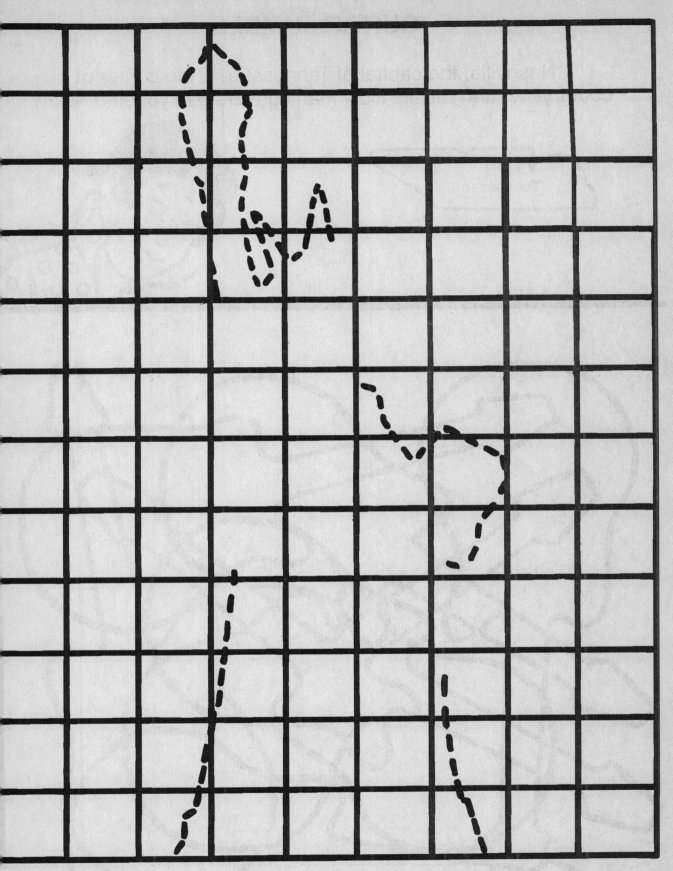

aw the Statue of Liberty. Use the dashed lines as guides and draw the lines in each square on this page by looking at each square on the opposite page.

GUITAR JUMBLE

Nashville, the capital of Tennessee, is the center of country-western music. How many guitars can you find below?

Tennessee

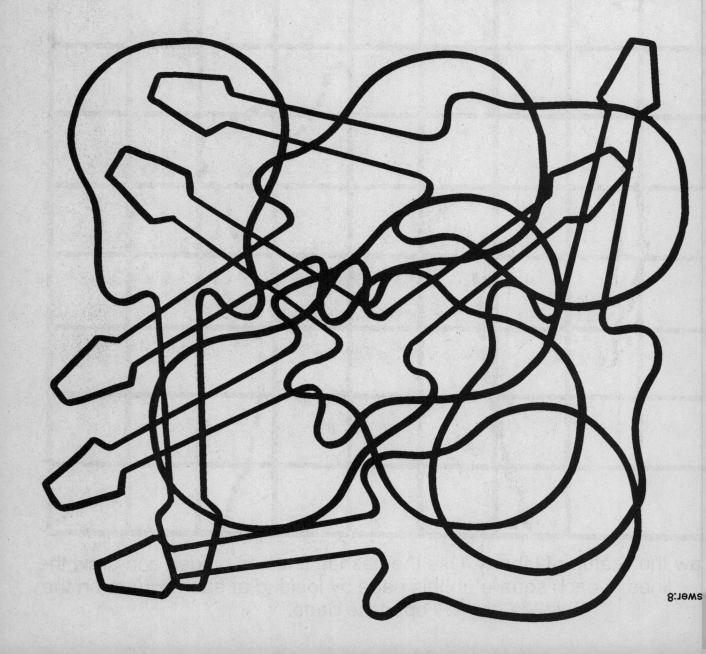

Texas

TEXAS COLORING FUN

Texas is the foremost cowboy and cattle state.
It leads all states in the production of beef cattle.

UTAH DOT TO DOT

Utah

Utah was the site where the golden spike was driven, joining the East and West coast. **Follow the dots** to see what the first cross-country train looked like.

MAPLE SYRUP MAZE
Vermont is known for its maple syrup.
Three million maple trees per year are tapped for syrup.
Which bucket will the syrup be dropped in?

STAR FIND

Virginia is known as the "Mother of Presidents,"
because 8 presidents were born there.
Can you find 8 stars below?

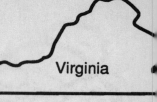

Virginia

WEST VIRGINIA C'S

West Virginia supplies 30% of the nation's coal. Coal starts with the letter C. Find **12** items in the picture above that begin with the letter C.

W.Virginia

PENNSYLVANIA LIBERTY

Pennsylvania

On July 4, 1776, the Declaration of Independence was signed in Philadelphia, Pennsylvania. Which rope rings the Liberty Bell?

WYOMING

Dude ranches were started in Wyoming. Color by Number
to see what the dude is doing wrong.
1—Brown 2—Yellow 3—White 4—Blue 5—Green

WISCONSIN DAIRY JUMBLE

Wisconsin is the nation's leading producer of milk, cheese and butter. How many of each can you find in the jumble above?

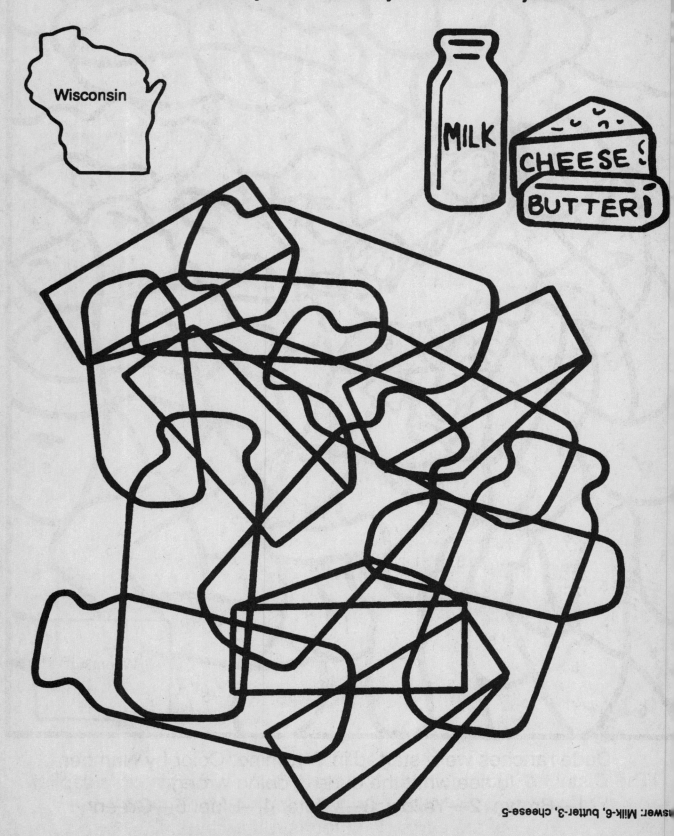

Wisconsin

MILK

CHEESE

BUTTER

DOT TO DOT FUN!

The District of Columbia is not a state, but it is the nation's capital.
Follow the dots to see the Washington Monument—one
of the city's great tourist attractions.

Now that you have learned some facts about the states,
see if you can draw your state in the space above.